JUL   2009

BARACK OBAMA

OUR FORTY-FOURTH PRESIDENT

by Catherine Nichols

THE CHILD'S WORLD®

Published in the United States of America

The Child's World®
1980 Lookout Drive • Mankato, MN 56003-1705
800-599-READ • www.childsworld.com

Acknowledgments
The Child's World®: Mary Berendes, Publishing Director

Creative Spark: Mary McGavic, Project Director; Melissa McDaniel, Editorial
Director; Deborah Goodsite, Photo Research

The Design Lab: Kathleen Petelinsek, Design; Gregory Lindholm, Page Production

Content Adviser: David R. Smith, Adjunct Assistant Professor of History,
University of Michigan–Ann Arbor

Photos
Cover and page 3: Emmanuel Dunand/AFP/Getty Images

Interior: Associated Press Images: 4 and 38, 12 and 38, 17 (Obama Presidential
Campaign), 9 (SDN School Menteng 1), 10 (Lucy Pemoni), 11, 18, 26 (Obama
for America), 13 (Marco Garcia), 37 (Associated Press Photo); Corbis: 19 (Joe
Wrinn/Harvard University/Handout), 20 (Radu Sigheti/Reuters), 23 (John Gress);
Getty Images: 7 (Keystone Features), 21 (Scott Olson), 27 (Nam Y. Huh-Pool),
28, 32 and 39 (Tim Boyle), 29 (Spencer Platt), 30 (Brendan Smialowski/AFP), 36
and 39 (Justin Sullivan); iStockphoto: 44 (Tim Fan); Landov: 5, 8 (Obama Press
Office/UPI Photo), 22 (Obama For America/Reuters), 24 (Brian Kersey/UPI),
33 (Paul Moseley/MCT), 34 (Tim Shaffer/Reuters); Photo Courtesy of Punahou
School: 15; U.S. Air Force photo: 45.

Library of Congress Cataloging-in-Publication Data
Nichols, Catherine.
  Barack Obama / by Catherine Nichols.
     p. cm. — (Presidents of the U.S.A.)
  Includes index.
  ISBN 978-1-60253-072-0 (library bound : alk. paper)
  1. Obama, Barack—Juvenile literature. 2. Legislators—United
States—Biography—Juvenile literature. 3. Presidential candidates—
United States—Biography—Juvenile literature. 4. African American
legislators—Biography—Juvenile literature. 5. United States. Congress.
Senate—Biography—Juvenile literature. 6. Racially mixed people—United
States—Biography—Juvenile literature. I. Title. II. Series.

E901.1.O23N534 2008
328.73092—dc22
  [B]

2008045316

Barack Obama was elected president in 2008.

TABLE OF CONTENTS

CHAPTER ONE

A MULTICULTURAL CHILDHOOD

For many years, Barack Obama struggled to make sense of his **multicultural heritage.** He is the son and grandson of people who came from Kansas in the center of the United States. He is also the son and grandson of people who came from a small village in Kenya in East Africa. He grew up in Honolulu, Hawaii, and Jakarta, Indonesia.

Barack Obama was born in Hawaii. Here, he plays on the beach with his grandfather, Stanley Dunham.

*Barack's mother,
Ann Dunham, was
born in Kansas.
She and her parents
moved to Hawaii in
1960, a year after
it became a state.*

Barack's mother, a young woman named Ann Dunham, had moved from Kansas to Hawaii with her family during her teen years. Barack's father, who was also named Barack Obama, had a different story. As a boy, he had tended goats in his father's village in Kenya. Obama Sr. did well at school, and he received a **scholarship** to study at the University of Hawaii. That's where the two young people met and fell in love. They married in 1960, and on August 4, 1961, their son was born.

When Barack was two years old, his father was offered a scholarship to study at Harvard University in Massachusetts. The scholarship would pay for school and his expenses, but included no money to support his family. Obama Sr. was ambitious. He felt he couldn't turn down such an offer. He left for Harvard, while Barack and his mother stayed behind in Hawaii. Barack would not see his father again for eight years.

The name Honolulu comes from two words in Hawaiian: *hono*, "a joining together," and *lulu*, "a shelter from the wind." People from many backgrounds have joined together to make this city. Some have roots in China, Japan, and the Philippines. Others moved to Hawaii from the **mainland** United States.

Barack's mother's full name was Stanley Ann Dunham. She was given the name Stanley by her father, who had hoped (before she was born) that she would be a boy. She went by her middle name, Ann.

Barack means "blessed" in Arabic.

Toot is short for *tutu*, the Hawaiian word for "grandmother."

Barack was close to his mother. She always made him feel special. She taught him to have **empathy** for other people. If he did or said something thoughtless or unkind, she'd ask, "How would that make you feel?" She also had a great sense of wonder—about people, paintings, poetry, music, and nature. When they walked together in the evening, she'd tell Barack to close his eyes and listen to the rustling leaves. Sometimes she'd wake him in the middle of the night to look at an especially bright and beautiful moon.

Barack was also close to his grandparents, Madelyn and Stanley Dunham. He called his grandmother "Toot." His grandfather was "Gramps." Barack remembers going swimming and spearfishing with Gramps in the sparkling waters around Honolulu. Once they went to Hickam Air Force Base to watch astronauts return from space. Barack sat on his grandfather's shoulders to get a good view.

In 1964, Barack's mother filed for divorce from his father, and she soon married again. Her new husband, Lolo Soetoro, came from the country of Indonesia. He was in Hawaii as a student.

In 1965, some Indonesians rebelled against their government. The Indonesian government then required all Indonesian students studying abroad to return home. In 1967, six-year-old Barack moved with his mother and new stepfather to Jakarta, the capital of Indonesia.

Indonesia was a poor country. Many people lived in mud and brick huts. They washed themselves and

their clothing in the river. There were few cars in the country. Instead, many people rode bicycles that pulled **rickshaws.** Barack's family lived in a small house on the edge of the city. The house had no air-conditioning, no refrigerator, and no flushing toilet. Barack's mother and stepfather couldn't afford to send him to one of the special schools where most American children in Jakarta went. Instead, he went to the local school with Indonesian children. In first grade, Barack wrote an essay. It was called "I Want to Become President." Barry, as everybody called him, was full of dreams for the future even then.

Obama lived in Jakarta, Indonesia, from 1967 to 1971. It was an exciting city filled with sights and sounds that were new to him.

Nine-year-old Barack Obama poses with his stepfather, mother, and younger sister, Maya. His stepfather, Lolo Soetoro, was a quiet, easygoing man who worked for an oil company.

Indonesia was a wonderful place for an adventurous young child. Barack had lots of new experiences and explored many new places. He remembers, "days of chasing down chickens and running from water buffalo, nights of shadow puppets and ghost stories and street vendors bringing . . . sweets to our door." Alligators, ducks, and chickens lived in his yard.

Best of all was Tata, a gibbon that played in the trees overhead. His stepfather had brought the wild ape all the way from the island of New Guinea as a gift for Barack. Soetoro treated Barack like a son. Once he bought him boxing gloves and taught him how to defend himself.

Barack made friends among the Indonesian children. He liked to show them the book about Disneyland that his grandmother had sent him. They also liked to look through a catalog from the United States, admiring all the wonderful things there were to buy. Though Barack lived like an Indonesian, he realized he was an American, too. And he realized something else. No one in the catalog looked like him. All the people in the photographs, even Santa Claus, were white.

Barack's mother taught her son to be proud of his heritage as an African American. She told him about people like Martin Luther King Jr., one of the leaders of the effort to gain **civil rights** for all Americans. She also worried that her son wasn't getting the education he needed. She sent to the United States for teaching materials. She woke Barack up every morning at four o'clock and spent three hours teaching him. Barack grumbled sometimes. "This is no picnic for me either, buster," his mother said.

In Indonesia, Barack tasted many foods that were new to him, including snake and grasshopper. He has said that snake meat is tough and that roasted grasshoppers are crunchy.

Barack Obama (circled) attended a neighborhood school in Jakarta. Classes were taught in Indonesian, so his mother made him get up early to do extra homework in English.

While she lived in Jakarta, Barack's mother worked teaching English to Indonesians.

Finally, Barack's mother decided that he would get a better education in Hawaii. When he was ten, she took him back to Honolulu to live with his grandparents and attend Punahou (Poon-a-ho) School. It was an expensive private school with an excellent reputation. Most of the students were of European or Asian background and came from well-known and well-to-do families. Barack's grandparents worked hard to help send him there.

On his first day at his new school, Barack's teacher introduced him to the other students in his class. They laughed at his unusual name. When they found out that his father came from Kenya, they made jokes. From then on, the other kids weren't mean to him.

Obama sometimes felt out of place at the Punahou School (right) because many of the students came from wealthy families.

*Barack Obama Sr. visited Hawaii when Barack was ten years old. Obama Sr. worked as an **economist** for the government in his home country of Kenya.*

They just ignored him. He was too different. He didn't even play the same games. He had learned to play soccer and badminton in Jakarta. He didn't know how to play football or ride a skateboard like the Hawaiian kids. Most days, Barack went right home after school to read comics or watch TV by himself.

At Christmas that year, he had a surprise visitor— his father, Barack Obama Sr. He came to Hawaii to see his son and to recover from a car accident. Barack barely remembered him. But he had heard about him. Barack's mother wanted her son to be proud of his father and his heritage. She told him that his father was an important leader in Kenya, who worked to help people improve their lives. Barack also learned that he had half-brothers and a half-sister he had never met.

At first, father and son were uncomfortable with each other. Once, Barack's father ordered him to turn off the TV and study. Barack ran into his room and

Barack's father belonged to Luo **ethnic group** in Kenya. It is the nation's third-largest ethnic group.

Obama lived with his grandparents throughout high school. Stanley Dunham was a furniture salesman. Madeyln Dunham worked at a bank and in 1970 became one of the first female bank vice presidents in Hawaii.

slammed the door. Barack's teacher invited his father to give a talk. Barack was afraid the other students would tease him even more. Obama Sr. spoke of the wild animals that ran free in his country. He told of young boys who had to kill a lion to prove they were men. He told of Kenya's long years of struggle to be free. The class was impressed. One boy who had teased Barack said, "Your dad is pretty cool." At the end of the month, Obama Sr. returned to Kenya. Barack would never see him again.

Soon after, Barack's mother and stepfather separated. She returned to Honolulu with his half-sister, Maya. Barack moved into an apartment with them. A few years later, his mother returned to Indonesia to study **anthropology.** Barack chose to stay behind with Toot and Gramps.

HAWAII AND INDONESIA

Barack Obama grew up on two islands—Oahu in Hawaii and Java in Indonesia. Hawaii is located in the Pacific Ocean about 2,500 miles (4,000 km) west of California. Indonesia is in Southeast Asia. It lies north of Australia between the Indian and Pacific oceans. Both Indonesia and Hawaii are warm year-round.

Barack Obama calls Indonesia "a nation of islands." In fact, it includes more than 17,000 islands. Some of the largest are Java, Sumatra, Sulawesi, and Bali. Hawaii could be called "a state of islands." It has hundreds. The main ones are Kauai, Oahu, Molokai, Lanai, Maui, and the largest of all, Hawaii, often called "the Big Island." Obama lived in Honolulu, the capital of Hawaii, and in Jakarta, Indonesia's capital.

Indonesia has more than 230 million people. Only China, India, and the United States are home to more people. Indonesians belong to many different ethnic groups and speak more than 700 languages. For about 350 years, the Dutch ruled Indonesia. After World War II, Indonesia became an independent country. Hawaii has about 1.3 million people of different backgrounds. It was an independent country until 1898, when the United States took it over. In 1959, Hawaii became the 50th state. In the picture above, Obama walks with his daughters on a beach in Hawaii.

CHAPTER TWO

DREAMS FROM HIS FATHER

Barack enjoyed his six years at Punahou School. The campus was beautiful. The other students were relaxed and easy to talk to once they got to know him. They called him Barry. He hung out with his many friends. He played on the school's championship basketball team, although he spent more time on the bench than he liked. He enjoyed reading and singing in the school choir.

But Barack's teen years were not perfect. For one thing, he missed his mother and Maya. He saw them only a few times a year. And he didn't always like following his grandfather's rules, such as filling the gas tank when he borrowed the car. He'd argue, listing reasons the rules weren't fair. Because he was good at arguing, he often left Gramps with nothing to say.

After awhile, Barack began to see things from his grandfather's point of view. He thought of the struggles Gramps had gone through and of his need to feel respected in his own home. "I recognized," Barack wrote, "that sometimes he really did have a point, and that in insisting on my own way all the

time, without regard to his feelings or needs, I was in some way **diminishing** myself." This was the empathy that Barack's mother had tried to teach him. Now he was beginning to understand it for himself. Empathy would become, Obama says, a "**guidepost** for my **politics.**"

Although Barack made friends at school, he sometimes felt like an outsider. Very few students there were African American. He became friendly with an older student who also had a multicultural background. The two young men had long talks. "Growing up," Obama has said, "I wasn't always sure who I was or what I was doing." He was trying to find out.

At Punahou School, Barack (top row) was considered a good-natured person who got along with everyone. Here, he poses with his fifth-grade class.

Under apartheid, the South African government put people into different racial categories. Black South Africans couldn't live in the same areas, hold the same jobs, or go to the same schools as white South Africans. Thanks to the efforts of leaders such as Nelson Mandela, South Africa's law of racial separation ended in February of 1991.

At Occidental College, Obama gave up the name Barry and told his fellow students to call him Barack.

Barack graduated from high school in 1979. By this time, he had chosen to attend Occidental College, a small college in Los Angeles, California, because a girl he liked was enrolling there. At age 18, Barack went to live on the United States mainland for the first time in his life.

Barack did well at Occidental. He enjoyed himself and made new friends. He also got involved in politics for the first time. When students on campus held a rally against **apartheid,** a racist policy in South Africa, he was one of the speakers.

Occidental was a small college. After attending for two years, Barack was ready to stretch his wings and see more of the world. He applied and was accepted to Columbia University in New York City.

At Columbia, Barack majored in **political science.** He had become more serious about his studies. He turned down invitations to parties in order to stay home and study. The rest of the time he explored the city. He saw skyscrapers being built and streets full of people with plenty of money to spend in dazzling shops. He also saw abandoned buildings in poor neighborhoods, people sleeping on the sidewalk, and people who sold drugs openly on the street.

Soon after Barack graduated in 1983, he received a telephone call from Kenya. His father had been killed in an automobile accident. Barack hardly knew how he should feel. He hadn't seen his father since that month-long visit ten years before. He had written letters and received some back, but the letters had

grown fewer and fewer on both sides over the years. Still his father, his father's family, and his father's country were all somehow part of him. How could Barack know who he was, if he didn't know them? He vowed that someday he would travel to Kenya and learn more about that part of himself.

But Barack Obama knew he was not a Kenyan. He was an American. He longed for a place to live in America where he could put down roots and feel at home. He also wanted to find work to do that would be useful and help people. Obama decided to move to Chicago, Illinois, and become a community organizer. He would try to help poor people come together to help themselves.

Obama moved to New York City in 1981 to attend Columbia University. He studied hard during his two years there.

COMMUNITY ORGANIZING

Community organizers help people in a community come together to solve their problems. They might work with renters' groups worried about large rent increases on their apartments, or bus riders unable to get to work because bus service has been cut back. They might help poor people organize to keep a neighborhood grocery store open.

Community organizers don't solve people's problems. Instead, they teach people how to solve problems for themselves. Organizers show people how to run meetings, how to be comfortable speaking in public, and how to reach agreements with landlords, employers, and politicians. Organizers knock on doors to meet the people in their community. They encourage people to vote and to come to meetings to discuss their problems and figure out how to solve them. They work to bring groups together to get to know each other and help each other out.

Community organizing isn't easy. The pay is low and the hours are long. Organizers have to be good at listening to what other people say. They have to remember that their job is to help others learn to lead, not to be leaders themselves. But many people find the job satisfying because they are helping improve people's lives. The picture below shows Obama working as a community organizer in Chicago.

After trying for six months, he finally got a job with the Developing Communities Project, a church-based community organization on Chicago's South Side. This was a run-down section of the city. Some people in the community were discouraged. Jobs had disappeared. Housing was badly in need of repair. Obama didn't earn much money at his job as a community organizer, but he didn't care. He discovered he was good at talking to people and getting them to trust him. He got people to work together to get what they needed.

Three years later, Obama was ready to move on. He was proud of what he'd accomplished, but he wanted to do more. "The victories were small," says a man he worked with. "They changed people's lives, but they didn't change American society and he wanted to do that."

At age 26, Obama was accepted to Harvard Law School in Cambridge, Massachusetts. It is one of the most respected law schools in the country. At Harvard,

Obama began attending Harvard Law School in 1988. He would graduate in 1991 with high honors.

Obama visited Kenya for the first time in 1988. Here he is shown on a return visit with his arm around his step-grandmother, Sarah Obama.

he could acquire the knowledge, friends, and power to bring about real change. A Harvard education, Obama has said, "means you can take risks. You can try to do things and still land on your feet."

During these years, Obama remained close to his family. His stepfather died in 1987. After that, his relationship with his half-sister, Maya, changed. He "really took on the role of a father," she says. He didn't forget his own father, either. Before entering law school, Obama finally made the journey to Kenya that he'd promised himself.

Obama met many relatives in Kenya—a step-grandmother, half-brothers, a half-sister, aunts, uncles, and cousins. He got to know these family members he had never met before. They took him on a journey to the home in the country where his grandparents had lived. When Obama saw his father's grave, he knelt and wept. He was sad, but he was at peace. With a stronger sense of who he was, he could get on with his life.

CHAPTER THREE

ENTERING POLITICS

The summer after his first year in law school, Obama got a summer job as an **intern** at a Chicago law firm. A young woman named Michelle Robinson was assigned to be his adviser. She had gone to law school right after college and was already working as a lawyer.

Barack liked Michelle very much, and he began asking her out on dates. Michelle refused. She felt it wasn't appropriate since she was his adviser. Eventually, she agreed. They began their relationship sitting on a curb eating ice cream cones. They continued their relationship after Obama went back to Harvard. In his second year of law school, he was elected president of the *Harvard Law Review*. He was the first African American to receive this honor.

Barack Obama won his first political race in 1996.

The *Harvard Law Review* is one of the most respected legal journals in America. Presidents of the review have gone on to become university presidents, governors, and Supreme Court justices.

After graduating from law school, Obama had two big decisions to make: where he should live and what kind of work he should do. The first decision was easy. He would move back to Chicago. He had come to feel at home in the city. He thought it was a good place to put down roots. Besides, that's where Michelle was. He knew he wanted to marry her. He also knew they would both want to live close to her family.

The second decision was pretty easy, too. The honor of being president of the law review had brought Obama lots of job offers. He decided to join a small Chicago law firm where he could work on civil rights cases.

Barack Obama and Michelle Robinson were married on October 18, 1992. Like her husband, Michelle Obama is a lawyer who went to Harvard Law School.

Barack and Michelle Obama have two children, Malia (left) and Sasha.

Obama also received offers from book publishers who thought Americans would be interested in his life story. They asked him to write his **autobiography.** His recent visit to Kenya was still strong in his mind. He set to work on a book about his experiences growing up as the child of a mother from Kansas and a father from Kenya. He called his book *Dreams from My Father.* The book was published in 1995. That same year, Obama's mother died of cancer at age 52.

Barack and Michelle married in October of 1992 in Chicago. Their first child, Malia was born in 1998. That summer, both parents took time off from work to enjoy their new baby. A few years later, in 2001, their second daughter, Natasha, was born. They call her Sasha for short.

Malia's name has two meanings. In Hawaiian, it means "calm." In Swahili, an African language, it means "queen."

MICHELLE OBAMA

Michelle Robinson grew up on Chicago's South Side. Her mother was a homemaker until Michelle and her older brother, Craig, grew up. Then she worked as a secretary in a bank. Michelle's father worked at a city water plant. He had a disease called multiple sclerosis. Although his condition grew worse over time, he continued to work and care for his family.

Michelle was an excellent student and a good basketball player. After high school, she went to Princeton University, and then, like Obama, she studied law at Harvard. In high school and college, Michelle pushed herself, expecting the most from herself and the people around her.

Michelle graduated from law school in 1988 and began working as an attorney at a law firm. After she married, Michelle left the law firm and took public service jobs in Chicago. Her last position was as a vice president at the University of Chicago Hospitals. In 2007, she decided to cut back her hours to help with her husband's campaign.

Michelle Obama spoke on the first night of the 2008 Democratic National Convention. She told the audience that she and her husband believed "that you work hard for what you want in life, that your word is your bond, and you do what you say you're going to do, that you treat people with dignity and respect, even if you don't know them, and even if you don't agree with them."

Obama worked as a lawyer for several years. He also taught **constitutional** law at the University of Chicago for 12 years. "I loved the law school classroom," Obama says. He enjoyed teaching about the United States **Constitution** because he believes it shapes American attitudes. Obama points out that despite their many differences of opinion, Americans agree on the importance of personal liberty and the basic rules of **democracy.** They believe they have the freedom to speak their minds, to worship as they see fit, to buy and own property, to live their lives as they want. All these freedoms are spelled out in the Constitution.

Obama decided to enter politics. There was an opening in the Illinois state senate. He'd worked as a community organizer and a civil rights lawyer. He felt that perhaps he could do even more as a state senator. After talking it over with Michelle, he entered the race. He won the election.

During his time in the state senate, Obama was able to accomplish many things. He helped expand health care for children and change the state's death penalty system. But he was not successful in everything he tried. In 2000, he ran for a seat in the U.S. House of Representatives against Democratic congressperson Bobby Rush.

Rush was well known; Obama was not. At one point in the campaign, Rush got a lot of sympathy when one of his sons was shot and killed. Over the Christmas holidays, the state legislature was called back to vote on a gun control law. Obama was in Hawaii with his wife and baby daughter visiting his grandmother. He couldn't get back in time to vote because Malia was too sick to fly. The new law was defeated by just a few votes. Obama knew then that he was not going to be elected. To the media and the voters, he'd been enjoying himself on a tropical vacation when he should have been voting.

Despite his defeat, Obama didn't lose his interest in politics. In 2003, he decided to run for the U.S. Senate. First, he had to win the Democratic **primary.** This would take a lot of money, mainly to buy TV ads so that Illinois voters would know who he was and what he stood for. Another **candidate** for the seat was wealthy and could pay for his own campaign. Obama was not wealthy, so he had to ask other people for money. Fund-raising, as it is called, is a big part of the election process. It was the part Obama liked least.

Obama worked as a professor at the University of Chicago Law School for 12 years. He taught part-time, while also holding other jobs.

He remembered his grandfather telling him about when he worked as an insurance salesman. His grandfather hated having to call people he didn't know and ask them to buy insurance. "More than ever," Obama says, "I understood how my grandfather must have felt." Despite his dislike of fund-raising, Obama won the primary.

That same year, John Kerry, a senator from Massachusetts, was the Democratic candidate for president. Obama spoke at some of Kerry's campaign events and impressed Kerry. One day, Obama got a phone call while riding in a car. Kerry wanted him to give the **keynote address** at the Democratic Convention. After he hung up, Obama turned to the an aide, Mike Signator, and said, "I guess this is pretty big." Signator nodded. "I guess you could say that." It was bigger news than Obama realized.

As he planned his speech, Obama thought about what many politicians were saying. They claimed that

*In 2004, Obama competed against **Republican** Alan Keyes (right) for a seat in the U.S. Senate. It was the first U.S. Senate race ever in which both the Republican and the Democratic candidates were African American.*

During his campaign for the U.S. Senate, Obama talked to people all across Illinois. Here, he talks with a restaurant owner about the problems she faces.

America was divided. They said Americans didn't have much in common anymore. Different groups of people held different beliefs. People disagreed strongly with each other. They didn't understand people who came from different backgrounds.

Obama remembered the Americans he had met while campaigning. Some had told him of their efforts to succeed despite setbacks and hardships. No matter how impossible their dreams, they dared to keep on hoping. He also remembered a sermon given by the minister of his church, Jeremiah A. Wright Jr. In this sermon, Wright talked about the "**audacity** of hope."

Obama liked that phrase. That's what the people whose stories he'd heard had shown. It's what Americans have always shown. It's what drew them together, despite their differences. He decided to give a speech about the audacity of hope.

CHAPTER FOUR

THE AUDACITY OF HOPE

On July 27, 2004, Barack Obama stood up before the Democratic National Convention. Unlike most of the speakers that night, the slender young African American man was not a well-known politician. Many people who listened to him that night had not heard of him before and did not know what to expect. But then Obama began to speak. His voice was easy to listen to. It was strong and powerful, yet friendly.

Obama's words struck a chord with many of his listeners. He talked about what united Americans, not about what divided them. "There is not a black America and white America and Latino America and Asian America— there's the United States of America," he said.

Obama made a big impression on the people who saw and heard him. Interest was growing in the "skinny

Obama speaking at the Democratic Convention in 2004

Obama won election to the Senate with 70 percent of the vote. It was the largest victory for a statewide race in Illinois history.

Obama was the fifth African American ever to serve in the U.S. Senate.

Obama speaks to Delaware senator Joseph Biden in the Capitol in 2005. Obama would later choose Biden to be the Democratic vice-presidential candidate.

guy with the funny name," as he liked to call himself. Some people were even saying he might be the next president of the United States.

After the convention, Obama returned to Illinois, and in November, he won his election to the U.S. Senate. Obama moved into his new office in January of 2005. He and Michelle had decided it would be better for their daughters if they kept their home base in Chicago. Obama rented a small apartment for the nights he would stay in Washington. He settled in to learn his new job.

For two years, Obama was very busy. He **sponsored bills,** worked on **committees,** traveled to eastern Europe, the Middle East, and Africa. Along with former presidents Bill Clinton and George H. W. Bush, he went to New Orleans, Louisiana, to get help for the victims of Hurricane Katrina. Obama worked to make health care affordable and improve education. He was involved with issues of protecting the environment. He planned a way to end the U.S. war in Iraq peacefully. He also kept in touch with the voters of Illinois to answer their questions and listen to their concerns.

In 2006, Obama published his second book. He called it *The Audacity of Hope: Thoughts on Reclaiming the American Dream.* In the book, he wrote about the things that he thought were right with America and the things that he thought were wrong. He explained that Americans may seem divided, but they all believe in the ideas contained in the Declaration of Independence. Among these, Obama wrote, were the ideas "that we are born into this world free . . . ; that each of us arrives with a bundle of rights that can't be taken away . . . ; [that] we can, and must, make of our lives what we will."

Obama believed that government could help people make the best use of their rights and freedoms. He believed three issues were the most important: ending the war in Iraq, ensuring that all Americans have affordable health care, and having the United States produce more of its own energy. As a senator,

Obama filled his office in Washington with photographs of his heroes. They include President Abraham Lincoln, civil rights leader Martin Luther King Jr., South African president Nelson Mandela, President John F. Kennedy, and boxer Muhammad Ali. They also include Thurgood Marshall, the first African American to sit on the U.S. Supreme Court, and Indian leader Mahatma Gandhi, who argued that people should struggle nonviolently against things that are wrong in society.

Obama signs copies of his book The Audacity of Hope. *The book sold more than a million copies.*

he could work on these issues. But he would have more power to make change if he were president. On a cold day in February of 2007, Obama stood in front of the Old State Capitol Building in Springfield, Illinois, and announced he was running for president. "I know I haven't spent a lot of time learning the ways of Washington," he said. "But I've been there long enough to know that the ways of Washington must change."

Change was the rallying cry of Obama's campaign to win the Democratic **nomination** for president. His main rival in the primaries was Senator Hillary Rodham Clinton from New York. Clinton was well known, both as a senator and as the wife of former president Bill Clinton. Experience was her rallying cry. She claimed that she had it and Obama didn't.

The primaries were hard fought. Obama won in some states. Clinton won in others. Obama raised a record-breaking amount of money for his campaign. Much of the money came from people who contributed less than $200 each. This was partly due to Obama's ease and skill with the Internet. He attracted the interest and enthusiasm of many young people.

Both Obama and Clinton were pioneering candidates. No woman or African American had ever been president of the United States. Many people wondered if Americans were ready to elect a woman president or a black president. "I absolutely think America is ready," Obama said. He had faith "that the American people—once they get to know you—are going to judge you on your individual character."

HIllary Clinton greets supporters at a campaign event in Texas.

John McCain and Sarah Palin were the Republican candidates for president and vice president in 2008.

In March, videos appeared of sermons delivered by Obama's pastor and friend, Jeremiah Wright. In them, Wright said angry things about the U.S. government and race in America. Many white people wondered if Obama felt the same. Obama decided to address the uncomfortable issue of race.

He gave a speech entitled "A More Perfect Union." Obama's multicultural background served him well when confronting the issue of race. So did his mother's teaching on empathy. He was able to understand how people of different races felt. He told white Americans about the hardships and **prejudice** a black man like Wright had endured in his life. He told black Americans that many whites also had hard lives and didn't like being blamed for what other white people had done in the past. Obama's speech was praised for its honesty and directness. Some said it was the most important speech of its time.

The primary race went down to the wire. By June 3, people in all the states had voted, and it was clear that Obama would be the Democratic candidate. This was made official two months later at the Democratic National Convention. Obama selected Senator Joseph Biden of Delaware to run for vice president.

The Democrats turned their attention to the general election. The Republican candidates were Senator John McCain of Arizona and Sarah Palin, the governor of Alaska. Age now became an issue in the campaign. If elected, John McCain, at age 72, would be the oldest president ever elected. Obama, at age 46, would be one of the youngest. Republicans claimed Obama didn't have enough experience to be president.

Many voters were concerned about the **economy** and the war in Iraq. Obama and McCain debated who would be best able to lead the United States at this difficult time. McCain said Obama didn't understand the main issues. Obama claimed McCain still supported policies that had failed.

By September, many people feared that the state of the nation's economy had become a crisis. Many banks and other large companies had made risky decisions in previous years. Now they were in danger of going out of business. People across the country were

Sarah Palin was the second woman to be the vice-presidential candidate of a major political party. The first was Geraldine Ferraro, the Democratic candidate for vice president in 1984.

Theodore Roosevelt was 42 years old when he became president, making him the youngest president in the nation's history. Ronald Reagan, the oldest president ever, was 69 when he became president. He served for eight years, leaving office at age 77.

worried about their jobs and savings. Many voters blamed the bad news on the Republicans in power. The Democratic candidate looked better and better.

More people cast votes in the 2008 presidential election than in any other. And when the votes were counted that night, history had been made. On November 4, 2008, Barack Obama became the first African American to be elected president of the United States. On election night, Obama stood before a crowd of more than 200,000 people in Chicago and spoke of the historic moment. He said, "If there is anyone out there who still doubts that America is a place where all things are possible, . . . tonight is your answer."

Supporters wave flags as Obama speaks to the nation the night he won the presidential election.

BREAKING BARRIERS: JOHN F. KENNEDY AND BARACK OBAMA

Barack Obama has been compared to another youthful president, John Fitzgerald Kennedy (shown above with his wife, Jacqueline). Both were in their first term in the U.S. Senate when they decided to run for president. Both had to overcome prejudice. Kennedy was the first Roman Catholic elected president. Obama was the first African American. Both inspired young people.

Kennedy, often called JFK, was born in Brookline, Massachusetts, in 1917. He served in the U.S. Navy in World War II. After the war, he became a U.S. representative from Massachusetts and then a senator. Kennedy won the 1960 presidential election, but he was president for less than two years. On November 22, 1963, he was shot and killed.

At the 2008 Democratic National Convention, Kennedy's younger brother, Senator Edward Kennedy of Massachusetts, said, "There was another time, when another young candidate was running for president and challenging America to cross a new frontier." He quoted his brother's words: "The world is changing. The old ways will not do."

Obama also called for change. "America is ready for a new set of challenges," he said. "This is our time. A new generation is prepared to lead."

TIME LINE

1961
On August 4, Barack Hussein Obama is born in Honolulu, Hawaii. He is the son of Stanley Ann Dunham from Kansas and Barack Obama from Kenya.

1963
Barack Obama Sr. enrolls in Harvard University in Massachusetts, leaving his wife and son in Hawaii.

1967
Now divorced, Barack's mother marries Lolo Soetoro, an Indonesian. The family moves to Jakarta, Indonesia.

1971
Obama returns to Hawaii to live with his grandparents and attend Punahou School. His father comes from Kenya for a visit and stays a month.

1979
Obama enters Occidental College in California.

1981
Obama transfers to Columbia University in New York City, where he majors in political science.

1983
Obama graduates from Columbia University.

1985
Obama begins working as a community organizer in Chicago, Illinois.

1988
Obama makes a month-long trip to Kenya to visit his relatives. When he returns, he enters Harvard Law School.

1990
Obama is elected president of the *Harvard Law Review,* becoming the first African American to receive this honor.

1991
Obama graduates from law school and returns to Chicago. He works as a civil rights lawyer and as a professor of constitutional law at the University of Chicago.

1992
Barack Obama marries attorney Michelle Robinson on October 18.

1995
Obama publishes his autobiography, *Dreams from My Father*. Obama's mother, Stanley Ann Dunham, dies at age 52.

1996
Obama wins election to the Illinois Senate.

2000
Obama campaigns for a seat in Congress but loses in the Democratic primary to Bobby Rush.

2004
Obama delivers the keynote address at the Democratic National Convention. On November 2, he is elected a U.S. senator.

2006
Obama's second book, *The Audacity of Hope*, is published.

2007
Obama announces he will run for president and begins his primary campaign.

2008
Obama narrowly defeats Senator Hillary Rodham Clinton of New York to become the Democratic presidential candidate. On November 4, Obama defeats Republican John McCain in the presidential election.

2009
Obama is sworn in as president on January 20.

GLOSSARY

anthropology (an-thruh-PAW-luh-jee)
Anthropology is the study of human
societies and cultures. Obama's mother
studied anthropology.

apartheid (uh-PAR-tayt) Apartheid was
a system of legal racial discrimination in
South Africa. Obama spoke out against
apartheid while he was a college student.

audacity (aw-DA-suh-tee) Audacity
is boldness or daring. Obama wrote a
book called *The Audacity of Hope*.

autobiography (aw-tow-by-AW-gruh-fee)
An autobiography is the story a person
writes about his or her own life. Obama's
autobiography is called *Dreams from
My Father*.

bills (BILZ) Bills are ideas for new laws. A bill
becomes law after both houses of Congress
pass the bill and the president signs it.

candidate (KAN-duh-dayt) A candidate
is a person who is running in an election.
At least two candidates run for president
every four years.

civil rights (SI-vul RYTZ) Civil rights are
the rights guaranteed by the Constitution
to all citizens of the United States. Obama
worked as a lawyer protecting civil rights.

committees (ku-MIH-teez) Committees are
groups of people who work on a particular
problem or issue. Obama worked on
many committees in the U.S. Senate.

Constitution (kon-stuh-TOO-shun) A
constitution is a set of basic principles
that govern a state, country, or society.
The U.S. Constitution promises
certain rights to American citizens.

constitutional (kon-stuh-TOO-shun-ul)
Something that is constitutional is related
to the Constitution. Obama taught
constitutional law at the University
of Chicago.

convention (kun-VEN-shun) A
convention is a meeting. The Democratic
and Republican political parties hold
national conventions every four years to
choose their presidential candidates.

democracy (deh-MAW-kruh-see) A
democracy is a country in which the
government is run by the people who live
there. The United States is a democracy.

Democratic (de-muh-KRAH-tik) If
something is Democratic, it is related
to the Democratic Party. Obama
gave the keynote address at the 2004
Democratic National Convention.

diminishing (duh-MIH-nish-ing) If
you're diminishing something, you're
making it become smaller or lessening its
dignity or reputation. Obama felt that if
he did not think about his grandfather's
feelings, he was diminishing himself.

economist (i-KAW-nuh-mist) An
economist is someone who is an expert
in the way money is earned and spent.
Obama's father was an economist.

economy (ee-KON-uh-mee) The
economy is the way money is earned
and spent in a country or area. During
the 2008 election, many Americans
were worried about the economy.

empathy (EM-puth-ee) Empathy is the
state of being aware of someone else's
feelings and experiences. Obama's mother
taught him the importance of empathy.

ethnic group (ETH-nik GROOP)
An ethnic group is a group of people
with common traits and customs and a
sense of shared identity. Obama's father
belonged to the Luo ethnic group.

generation (jen-uh-RAY-shun) A generation is a group of people born and living at the same time. Obama is part of a new generation of leaders.

guidepost (GYDE-post) A guidepost is a signpost or something that serves as a clue to a complicated issue. Obama considers empathy a guidepost to his politics.

heritage (HAYR-uh-tij) A person's heritage is the cultural traditions and other things of value that have been passed down through the generations. Obama has a multicultural heritage.

intern (IN-turn) An intern is a student who works at a job, often without pay, to gain experience. During law school, Obama spent a summer working as an intern at a Chicago law firm.

keynote address (KEE-note uh-DRES) A keynote address is the main speech given at a meeting. Obama gave the keynote address at the 2004 Democratic National Convention.

landlords (LAND-lordz) Landlords are people who own houses or apartments that they rent to other people. Community organizers help renters deal with landlords.

mainland (MAYN-land) The mainland is the main part of a continent or country as distinguished from an island. Obama lived on the U.S. mainland for the first time when he was 18.

multicultural (mul-tee-KULCH-uh-rul) If something is multicultural, it is related to diverse cultures or ethnic groups. Obama has a multicultural background.

multiple sclerosis (MUL-tuh-pul skluh-ROW-sis) Multiple sclerosis is a disease involving the brain and spinal cord that may lead to numbness, weak arms and legs, poor speech and vision, and tiredness. Michelle Obama's father had multiple sclerosis.

nomination (nom-uh-NAY-shun) If someone receives a nomination, he or she is chosen by a political party to run for an office. Obama won the Democratic nomination for president in 2008.

political science (puh-LIT-i-kul SY-ents) Political science is the study of government and politics. Obama studied political science at Columbia University.

politics (PAWL-uh-tiks) Politics refers to the actions and practices of the government. Obama's first job in politics was as a member of the Illinois state senate.

prejudice (PREJ-uh-dis) Prejudice is having a bad opinion about someone without good reason. As an African American, Obama had to overcome prejudice.

primary (PRY-mayr-ee) A primary is an election in which members of a political party nominate candidates for office. Obama's main rival during the primaries was Senator Hillary Rodham Clinton.

Republican (ri-PUB-li-kun) A Republican is someone who is a member of the Republican political party. John McCain is a Republican.

rickshaws (RIK-shawz) Rickshaws are small, light carriages on two wheels. There were many rickshaws in Indonesia.

scholarship (SKAWL-ur-ship) A scholarship is money given to help pay for a student's education. Obama's father received a scholarship to study at the University of Hawaii.

sponsored (SPAWN-surd) If a politician sponsored a bill, he or she proposed it and urged it to be passed. As a senator, Obama sponsored many bills.

THE UNITED STATES GOVERNMENT

The United States government is divided into three equal branches: the executive, the legislative, and the judicial. This division helps prevent abuses of power because each branch has to answer to the other two. No one branch can become too powerful.

EXECUTIVE BRANCH

PRESIDENT
VICE PRESIDENT
DEPARTMENTS

The job of the executive branch is to enforce the laws. It is headed by the president, who serves as the spokesperson for the United States around the world. The president signs bills into law and appoints important officials such as federal judges. He or she is also the commander in chief of the U.S. military. The president is assisted by the vice president, who takes over if the president dies or cannot carry out the duties of the office.

The executive branch also includes various departments, each focused on a specific topic. They include the Defense Department, the Justice Department, and the Agriculture Department. The department heads, along with other officials such as the vice president, serve as the president's closest advisers, called the cabinet.

LEGISLATIVE BRANCH

CONGRESS
*Senate and
House of Representatives*

The job of the legislative branch is to make the laws. It consists of Congress, which is divided into two parts: the Senate and the House of Representatives. The Senate has 100 members, and the House of Representatives has 435 members. Each state has two senators. The number of representatives a state has varies depending on the state's population.

Besides making laws, Congress also passes budgets and enacts taxes. In addition, it is responsible for declaring war, maintaining the military, and regulating trade with other countries.

JUDICIAL BRANCH

SUPREME COURT
COURTS OF APPEALS
DISTRICT COURTS

The job of the judicial branch is to interpret the laws. It consists of the nation's federal courts. Trials are held in district courts. During trials, judges must decide what laws mean and how they apply. Courts of appeals review the decisions made in district courts.

The nation's highest court is the Supreme Court. If someone disagrees with a court of appeals ruling, he or she can ask the Supreme Court to review it. The Supreme Court may refuse. The Supreme Court makes sure that decisions and laws do not violate the Constitution.

CHOOSING THE PRESIDENT

It may seem odd, but American voters don't elect the president directly. Instead, the president is chosen using what is called the Electoral College.

Each state gets as many votes in the Electoral College as its combined total of senators and representatives in Congress. For example, Iowa has two senators and five representatives, so it gets seven electoral votes. Although the District of Columbia does not have any voting members in Congress, it gets three electoral votes. Usually, the candidate who wins the most votes in any given state receives all of that state's electoral votes.

To become president, a candidate must get more than half of the Electoral College votes. There are a total of 538 votes in the Electoral College, so a candidate needs 270 votes to win. If nobody receives 270 Electoral College votes, the House of Representatives chooses the president.

With the Electoral College system, the person who receives the most votes nationwide does not always receive the most electoral votes. This happened most recently in 2000, when Al Gore received half a million more national votes than George W. Bush. Bush became president because he had more Electoral College votes.

THE WHITE HOUSE

The White House is the official home of the president of the United States. It is located at 1600 Pennsylvania Avenue NW in Washington, D.C. In 1792, a contest was held to select the architect who would design the president's home. James Hoban won. Construction took eight years.

The first president, George Washington, never lived in the White House. The second president, John Adams, moved into the house in 1800, though the inside was not yet complete. During the War of 1812, British soldiers burned down much of the White House. It was rebuilt several years later.

The White House was changed through the years. Porches were added, and President Theodore Roosevelt added the West Wing. President William Taft changed the shape of the presidential office, making it into the famous Oval Office. While Harry Truman was president, the old house was discovered to be structurally weak. All the walls were reinforced with steel, and the rooms were rebuilt.

Today, the White House has 132 rooms (including 35 bathrooms), 28 fireplaces, and 3 elevators. It takes 570 gallons of paint to cover the outside of the six-story building. The White House provides the president with many ways to relax. It includes a putting green, a jogging track, a swimming pool, a tennis court, and beautifully landscaped gardens. The White House also has a movie theater, a billiard room, and a one-lane bowling alley.

PRESIDENTIAL PERKS

The job of president of the United States is challenging. It is probably one of the most stressful jobs in the world. Because of this, presidents are paid well, though not nearly as well as the leaders of large corporations. In 2007, the president earned $400,000 a year. Presidents also receive extra benefits that make the demanding job a little more appealing.

★ **Camp David:** In the 1940s, President Franklin D. Roosevelt chose this heavily wooded spot in the mountains of Maryland to be the presidential retreat, where presidents can relax. Even though it is a retreat, world business is conducted there. Most famously, President Jimmy Carter met with Middle Eastern leaders at Camp David in 1978. The result was a peace agreement between Israel and Egypt.

★ *Air Force One:* The president flies on a jet called *Air Force One.* It is a Boeing 747-200B that has been modified to meet the president's needs.

Air Force One is the size of a large home. It is equipped with a dining room, sleeping quarters, a conference room, and office space. It also has two kitchens that can provide food for up to 50 people.

★ **The Secret Service:** While not the most glamorous of the president's perks, the Secret Service is one of the most important. The Secret Service is a group of highly trained agents who protect the president and the president's family.

★ **The Presidential State Car:** The presidential limousine is a stretch Cadillac DTS.

It has been armored to protect the president in case of attack. Inside the plush car are a foldaway desk, an entertainment center, and a communications console.

★ **The Food:** The White House has five chefs who will make any food the president wants. The White House also has an extensive wine collection.

★ **Retirement:** A former president receives a pension, or retirement pay, of just under $180,000 a year. Former presidents also receive Secret Service protection for the rest of their lives.

FACTS

QUALIFICATIONS

To run for president, a candidate must

* be at least 35 years old
* be a citizen who was born in the United States
* have lived in the United States for 14 years

TERM OF OFFICE

A president's term of office is four years.
No president can stay in office for more than two terms.

ELECTION DATE

The presidential election takes place every four years on the first Tuesday of November.

INAUGURATION DATE

Presidents are inaugurated on January 20.

OATH OF OFFICE

I do solemnly swear I will faithfully execute the office of the President of the United States and will to the best of my ability preserve, protect, and defend the Constitution of the United States.

WRITE A LETTER TO THE PRESIDENT

One of the best things about being a U.S. citizen is that Americans get to participate in their government. They can speak out if they feel government leaders aren't doing their jobs. They can also praise leaders who are going the extra mile. Do you have something you'd like the president to do? Should the president worry more about the environment and encourage people to recycle? Should the government spend more money on our schools? You can write a letter to the president to say how you feel!

1600 Pennsylvania Avenue
Washington, D.C. 20500
You can even send an e-mail to: president@whitehouse.gov

BOOKS

Devaney, Sherri, and Mark Devaney. *Barack Obama.*
Detroit: Lucent Books, 2007.

Dougherty, Steve. *Hopes and Dreams: The Story of Barack Obama.* New York: Black Dog & Leventhal, 2007.

Sapet, Kerrily. *Political Profiles: Barack Obama.* Greensboro, NC: Morgan Reynolds Publishing, 2008.

Thomas, Garen. *Yes We Can: Biography of Barack Obama.* New York: Feiwel and Friends, 2008.

Wagner, Heather Lehr. *Barack Obama.* New York: Chelsea House, 2008.

VIDEOS

The History Channel Presents: The Presidents. DVD (New York: A&E Home Video, 2005).

National Geographic's Inside the White House. DVD (Washington, DC: National Geographic Video, 2003).

INTERNET SITES

Visit our Web page for lots of links about
Barack Obama and other U.S. presidents:

http://www.childsworld.com/links

Note to Parents, Teachers, and Librarians: We routinely verify our Web links to make sure they are safe, active sites—so encourage your readers to check them out!